HIGHLAND COLLECTIONS

THE COLLECTIONS OF SEVEN 18th AND 19th
CENTURY FIDDLER-COMPOSERS FROM
THE HIGHLANDS OF SCOTLAND

William Christie, Cuminestown
Isaac Cooper, Banff
Angus Cumming, Grantown
Charles Grant, Knockando
Donald Grant, Elgin
James Henry, Garmond
William Morrison, Inverness

PUBLISHED IN 2005 BY

HIGHLAND
MUSIC
TRUST

Arras, Drumossie, Inverness IV2 5BB, Scotland

Tel: 01463 717811 Email: hmt@heallan.com

www.heallan.com

ISBN 0-9541478-4-7

Music set by Helen Allan   Project managed by Eric Allan
Advisers: Charles Gore & Duncan Dyker

Printed in Scotland by Dingwall Printers Ltd

PUBLISHERS' NOTE

Today's players and scholars have a hunger for good tunes from Scotland's past, to which they can give new life by letting them be heard again. Much of this valuable music has for long been available only in a small number of surviving copies of the originals, to be found in private hands or by patient research in libraries.

Our group of fiddler/composers is linked by a geographical thread, but their music, spanning a century, shows a variety of style, both in the original compositions and in the other dance tunes of the times which formed part of the compilers' repertoire.

In most cases, the bass lines were rudimentary, and we have omitted these except where they were clearly important to the arrangements. Otherwise, we have kept editorial interference to the minimum, making changes only to conform to present-day notation, or on occasion when the notes just "didn't add up".

We gratefully acknowledge the support for this publication from the AGR Findlay Charitable Trust, the Arts Council for Moray, the Gordon Fraser Charitable Trust, Highland Council, the Hope Scott Trust, the Scottish Arts Council and the family of the late Mrs Betty Grant, a lover of Scottish music. Thanks also go to all who have supported our work of "rescuing" some of Scotland's good music, and in particular to Charles Gore and Duncan Dyker for their goodwill and expertise.

HIGHLAND MUSIC TRUST is a Scottish charity, No SC028065, established for the advancement of education in and knowledge of Scottish national and traditional music. The proceeds of sale of this book will be used to continue the work of the Trust in making music available to all. Information on the Trust's publications may be had from the address on the previous page or the Trust's website www.heallan.com

---

CONTENTS

INTRODUCTION BY CHARLES GORE

THE COLLECTIONS   (each with index)

COMPOSITE INDEX

FIDDLER-COMPOSERS
OF THE EASTERN HIGHLANDS

Dancing and dance music were every bit as vigorous and popular in the eastern Highlands - Banff, Moray, Inverness - as in the rest of mainland Scotland in the 18th and 19th centuries. It is curious therefore that the actual published music of musicians of the region has suffered severe neglect, at any rate over the past century. While much of the music of the Gows of Athole and the Mackintoshes, along with some of their Edinburgh contemporaries, has fared better, some achieving later editions, that of William Christie, Isaac Cooper and William Morrison has not, with very few exceptions. This is not at all to suggest that their music is of a lesser quality, far from it. Some of their compositions would stand high in anyone's order of excellence. It was much more likely to have been due to reluctance on the part of music publishers of 100 years ago to publish whole editions of the older volumes.

As is evident from such massive compilations as *The Athole Collection*, Kerr's *"Merry Melodies"*, Glen's *Collection of Scottish Dance Music* and several others, they selected work from many of the old books. They were reacting to a genuine rebirth of interest in the tradition and their books became the seed-corn of the dance band repertoire of the 20th century, featuring between them at least a sample of the great talent of the Golden Age. The only trouble was that these compilers, for a reason which is now obscure, published almost every tune without any reference whatever to earlier or first editions, dates, composers, or other identifying information. As a result, later generations, who used those collections as "the bible" of traditional fiddle music for a hundred years, began to forget the original sources and to see the whole repertoire as "traditional", leaving the old books with their histories to fade into obscurity on library shelves. John Glen was in fact one of the few publishers of that era (1870 –1900) to include references to early editions. Even his useful efforts failed to gain lasting recognition…And so the moment when the older volumes might themselves have seen re-publication passed and was not destined to return until now, in the 21st. Century. The present generation has access to new editions distributed or published by Highland Music Trust.

The work of the seven fiddler-composers gathered into this new edition was first published over a period of about 100 years, from 1780 to1902. The music ranges from early examples of dance strathspeys with the accompanying reels and jigs popular in the late 18th century, right on to music composed in the closing years of the 19th century when James Scott Skinner was at the height of his career. They contain between them a feast of good music most of which has not been re-published elsewhere. The result is a net gain to the accessible repertoire of around 500 pieces, something the tradition hasn't experienced since Skinner's day. Highland Music Trust deserve the highest praise for their exertions in this field. The Athole Collection (re-published 1996) and Glen's Dance Music (2001) were seminal works in their day and are now widely available again; "The Mackintosh Collections" (2002) restore to full accessibility the work of one of Scotland's greatest fiddler-composers of the 18th century, Robert ("Red Rob") Mackintosh of Tulliemet and Edinburgh. All three editions are beginning to have their effect on the choice of music now in vogue and this in itself is a tribute to the fiddlers of the Golden Age.

WILLIAM CHRISTIE (1778 – 1849)

Dancing-master and fiddler-composer of Cuminestown, near Turriff, Aberdeenshire, Christie published in 1820 *"A Collection of Strathspeys, Reels, Hornpipes, Waltzes &c., arranged as medleys for the Harp, Piano Forte, Violin and Violoncello..."* Sixty-eight out of the 124 tunes published are his own compositions or arrangements; three others are attributed to John Christie (a brother or a son perhaps ?); the rest are either "Old", "Very Old" or "Irish". According to David Baptie ("Musical Scotland" 1894), he "was the first to popularise waltzes in the North of Scotland". One of his sons, another William, was a celebrated song collector ("Traditional Ballad Airs". 2 vols., 1876 & 1881) also remembered as Dean (for 30 years) of the Episcopal Diocese of Moray.

ISAAC COOPER (c 1755 – 1820)

A fiddler-composer and dancing-master in Banff, his first publication was *"Thirty New Strathspey Reels for the Violin or Harpsichord (1783, Banff & Edinburgh)"*. Another appeared around 1806/7: *"A Collection of Strathspeys, Reels and Irish Jigs...composed and selected by I. Cooper at Banff."* Cooper was a fine musician and, by all accounts, a prodigious teacher of music, not only of dancing, but also instruction "on the harpsichord or piano forte, violin, violincello, psaltery, clarionet, pipe and tabor, German flute, the Scots flute, the fife in the regimental style, the hautboy, the French Organ, the Irish Organ (bag) pipe; how to make flats, sharps and the proper chords with the brass keys; and the guitar …" ! If there is a single composition that secures him lasting fame it is "Miss Forbes' Farewell to Banff", set to words by John Hamilton, now perhaps forgotten, but the tune itself lives on a favourite to this day. Miss Forbes married (1788) James Urquhart of Meldrum, Sheriff of Banff for 51 years (1784-1835). Cooper married Miss Rebecca Reid, sister of Capt. Reid of Inverichnie (near Macduff) and is said to have died suddenly (c1811; Baptie says 1820) while playing his favourite tune, "Robin Adair", a tidy exit for a fiddler, poor but happy.

ANGUS CUMMING (c 1750 – c 1800)

Most of what is known about him can be gleaned from *"A Collection of Strathspey or Old Highland Reels by Angus Cumming at Grantown in Strathspey, 1780"* (Published in Edinburgh). Little else is known about Cumming except, as he makes clear in the book, he followed "the profession of his forefathers, who have been for many generations musicians in Strathspey". According to Thomas Newte Esq. *("Tour of England and Scotland", 1785/88)* "...the Cummings of Freuchie, now Castle Grant, were in the highest estimation for their knowledge and execution in Strathspey music, and most of the tunes handed down to us are certainly of their composing..." Newte also mentions John Roy Cumming as having died in the 1740s, but who was still remembered in the region as a performer of rare quality. Many other publishers of that time used the expression "Strathspey Reel", but the Cummings may have felt justified in claiming that their dynasty refined the dotted rhythm and gave it its uniquely Scottish identity in the field of dance. Although there is not a single claim to authorship by Cumming, it stands to reason that a proportion of the tunes are his. Equally, quite a number are not, either being of older vintage or widely published elsewhere.

CHARLES GRANT, M.A. (1807 – 1892)

For thirty years a schoolmaster in Aberlour, Speyside, where he was much admired for his music. Published after his death and printed privately, the collection of his tunes was quietly dipped into by the music researchers of RSCDS and then forgotten with the exception of the 6/8s "The Braes of Elchies", "Miss Jeannie S. Grant's Favourite" (used as the original tune for the dance "Two and Two", RSCDS Book 19) and "Mrs. Jamieson's Favourite", once played at dance tempo, now popular as a slow tune. There's a lot more to the collection than these! Grant has the distinction of having been a pupil of William Marshall and is said to have played some favourite strathspeys to the old man on his death-bed. In gratitude for this the family gave Grant Marshall's violin in 1851 (James Hunter). "A good executant upon the violin…", Mr. Grant was "esteemed as a cultured musician and on various occasions acted as judge at prize competitions." (Baptie)

DONALD GRANT (c 1760 – c 1835)

Fiddler-composer and dancing-master, born Elgin, c.1760 (he may have died there late in the 1830s, although proof is lacking that this was the same Donald Grant) leaving *"A Collection of Strathspeys, Reels, Jigs etc. . . "*, many of his own composition. It is dedicated to Mrs. Col. Grant of Grant. Originally published c 1790 in Edinburgh, every page of the edition I have seen (probably an 1820 reprint) is marked "Grant's 1st. Collection". But was there a second collection ? I have certainly never set eyes on it. . He is one of many of his kind who have left us tantalisingly little information about themselves. His dance teaching and music for social events would no doubt have taken him to Castle Grant, where he seems to have been well in with the family to whom he dedicates his work.

JAMES HENRY (1860 – 1914)

Born in Garmond, Aberdeenshire, Henry was leader of the Aberdeen Strathspey and Reel Society from its inception in 1903 until his death. His "Eight Airs for Violin" (price Two Shillings net) are just about all the musical history he left behind. The slow air "The Auld Brig o' Don "(aka the 13th century Brig o' Balgownie) was re-published by James Hunter in 1979. Another James Henry (or Hendry, 1877-1957)) a cobbler, who plied his trade in Macduff and Portsoy, may be the one described by Dr. Grant of Banff (*"Transactions of the Banffshire Field Club"*,1920-21) as "perhaps the finest living player of Scottish reels".

WILLIAM MORRISON (c 1780 – after 1825)

A native of Culloden, by Inverness, he published *"A Collection of Highland Music consisting of Strathspeys, Reels, Marches, Waltzes and Slow Airs with variations original and selected for the pianoforte, violin, violoncello...by William Morrison, J. Young & Co., ...Inverness ...(1812)"* It has 81 tune titles, about half of which are his own compositions, the remainder either old or by other composers of his time. One of his own tunes, a reel, bore the title: "Inverness or the Northern Meeting". Morrison provided the music for the Northern Meeting Balls for at least twelve years (1813 – 25), the first named bandleader to be appointed. The minutes of the Northern Meeting duly record that in 1820: "Mr. Morrison is engaged to take charge of the Ball Room music at the sum of £34.14/- being a good deal less than former years, with the usual allowance of porter to be given to the fiddles".(quoted in *"The Northern Meeting 1788-1988"* by Angus Fairrie, Inverness). He was succeeded by Joseph Lowe of Edinburgh, who continued in the post for 54 years.

William Marshall (1748 – 1831), born at Fochabers, Moray, a man of multiple natural talents, lived out his working life in the service of the Dukes of Gordon. Not all his music is well known but some of his lovely strathspeys, reels, jigs and slow tunes are popular in the contemporar y repertoire. As a native of Moray, he can rightly claim to be a Highlander, although his work is not "Gaelic" in any strict sense. It was published in Edinburgh and is closer in style to the other collections of dance music being published in central Scotland at the time, by such as Niel and Nathaniel Gow, Robert Mackintosh and a host of their contemporaries.

During the same era, rather by contrast, the *Reverend Patrick MacDonald* published (also in Edinburgh, in 1784) his *"Highland Vocal Airs"* in a deliberate attempt to "rescue" Gaelic music, until then a strictly oral tradition. He succeeded well with that work and *Captain Simon **Fraser**,* a native of Inverness-shire, added his *"Airs Peculiar to the Highlands and Islands of Scotland..."*, a curious hybrid work of traditional material and contemporary composition, much of it his own. The Gaelic titles that run through it often conflict with their English equivalents. It was first published in 1816 and re-published by his son Angus in 1874 and would even now benefit from more analysis and comment by Gaelic scholars. *Jane Fraser Morison*, of Kintail Manse, left two little collections of music of a generally "Gaelic" character in 1882, printed by Logan & Co., Inverness.

Any of these collections can be inspected and copies obtained (at a price) from one or more of Scotland's main libraries: The National Library of Scotland (Edinburgh), the Mitchell Library (Glasgow), the AK Bell Library (Perth), Dundee (The Wighton Collection) and Aberdeen Public Libraries and many of the university libraries. In the long-term it is to be hoped that all Scotland's traditional music will be made accessible on-line or in readily obtainable editions. In almost every case, the bequests of private collections (for example Glen and Wighton) were originally made on the understanding that the music should be freely accessible to all. Which means that it belongs, not to the libraries, but to the nation, and every musician has the right to demand free access to it.

Charlie Gore
Doune, Perthshire, Spring 2005

A
COLLECTION
OF
STRATHSPEYS, REELS, HORNPIPES, WALTZES, &c.
ARRANGED AS MEDLEYS
FOR THE
Harp
Piano Forte Violin and Violoncello
By
WILLIAM CHRISTIE,
Teacher of Dancing.

Ent. at Sta. Hall.

Price 3/

— EDINBURGH —

Printed for the Author, and to be had of him at Cuminestown by Turriff.

Also of Mr. Purdie N.º 10 Princes Street, Mess.rs Paterson & Robertson 13 Princes Street Edin.r

And Mr. Morris Union Street Aberdeen.

INDEX – WILLIAM CHRISTIE

Auchry

Wm Christie

Miss Garden Campbell of Troup's Hornpipe

Wm Christie

Sir Archd. Dunbar of Northfield's Strathspey

Wm Christie

Mr F G Campbell of Troup and Glenlyon's Reel

Wm Christie

When will ye wed me with a ring

Mrs Cumine of Auchry's Strathspey
Wm Christie

Lord Fife's Waltz
Wm Christie

Miss Robinson of Clermeston's Reel

Wm Christie

Miss Cumine of Auchry's Strathspey

Wm Christie

Let that stand there   -   a Reel

Old

Mr Gillan's Strathspey

Wm Christie

Slow when not danced

3

Mr Gillan's Reel

Wm Christie

Mrs Garden Campbell of Troup and Glenlyon's Strathspey

Old Gaelic Air

Very Slow when not Danced

cres.

cres.

cres.

Expn.

f

Communicated by Dr Stewart

Mrs Garden Campbell of Troup and Glenlyon's Reel

Wm Christie

The Right Honble. Lady Saltoun's Strathspey

Wm Christie

4

The Right Honble. Lady Saltoun's Reel

Wm Christie

Miss Dunbar of Northfield's Hornpipe *

Wm Christie

Allegretto

Dolce

p

f

* Now Mrs McIntosh of Raigmore

Mr Officer's Strathspey

Wm Christie

or

or

5

William's Love - a Reel

John Christie

The Punch is done * - a Jig

Old

Allegretto

* Communicated by Mr Jaffrey Senior

6

The Loch of Forfar   -   a Strathspey

Wm Allan

Dundarg   -   a Reel

Wm Christie

The Reel of the Mearn's

A Favorite Set

Strathspey Time

O if Jockey wou'd but steal me   -   a Reel

Old

Mormond   -   a Strathspey

Wm Christie

Mrs Gordon of Aberdour's Strathspey

Wm Christie

Mrs Dingwall of Brucklay's Reel

Wm Christie

Mrs Duff of Carnucie's Strathspey

Wm Christie

Mrs Duff of Carnucie's Reel

Wm Christie

The Smith he's black an' brucket

Old

Moderato

Communicated by J Allardyce

The Nine-Pint Coggie   a Reel

Old

FINE

D.C.

9

The Banks of the Deveron

Wm Christie

Slow

Dolce

Mrs Rose's Strathspey

Wm Christie

Dr Stewart's Reel

Wm Christie

Sarah Williamson's Lament

Very Old

Very Slow

Con Lamento

John Cumine Esqr of Auchry's Strathspey

Wm Christie

Miss Dunbar of Northfield's Favorite *   -   a Reel

John Christie

Now Mrs McIntosh of Raigmore

The Braes of Boyndlie

Old

Andante

My hearty wanton Carlie   -   a Strathspey   Old

Bonny Lassie turn you   -   a Reel   Old

FINE

D.C.

Mr Matthew's Strathspey   Wm Christie

12

Mr Matthew's Reel

Wm Christie

O what needs I my apron wash

Old

Andante

Amaroso

cres.

cres.

f

p

Mr Bruce's Strathspey

Wm Christie

Mr Bruce's Reel

Wm Christie

Willie's drown'd at Gamry

Old

Slow

Con Lamento   cres.   f

p   cres.   Expn.

Mrs Ernest Leslie's Strathspey

Wm Christie

The Rocks of Melross   -   a Reel

Wm Christie

My Bonny Laddie has my heart

Old

Slow and
Tender   cres.

cres.

p   Expn.

14

Mr Leid's Strathspey

Wm Christie

Mr Leid's Reel

Wm Christie

Mrs Dingwall of Brucklay's Waltz

Wm Christie

FINE

Minore

Dolce

D.C.

The Loch of Strathbeg   -   a Strathspey

Wm Christie

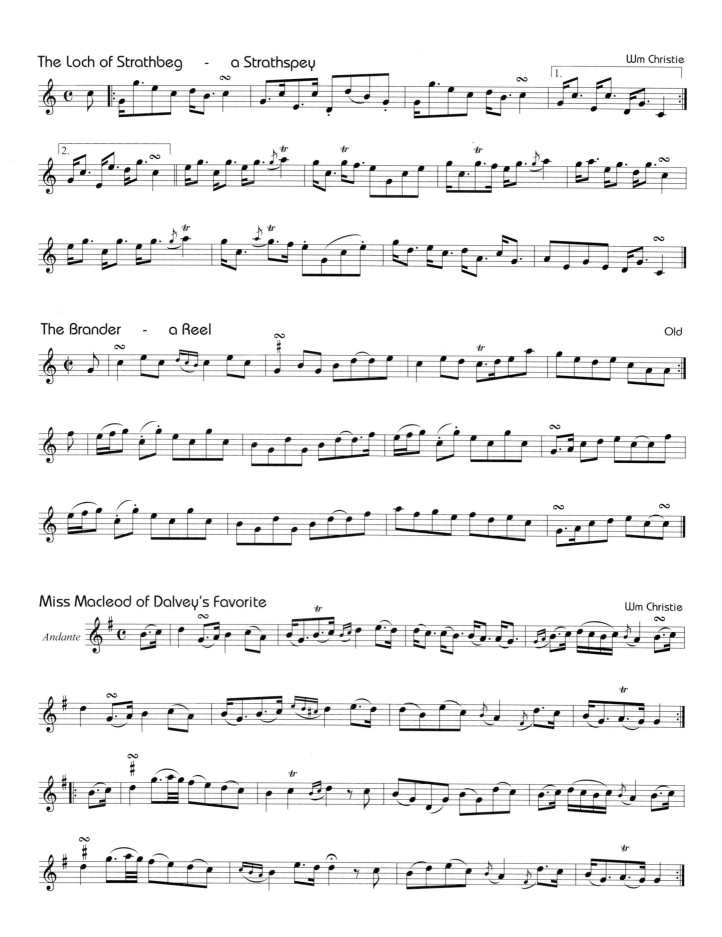

The Brander   -   a Reel

Old

Miss Macleod of Dalvey's Favorite

Wm Christie

Andante

Miss Macleod of Dalvey's Waltz

Wm Christie

Commin' thro' Kilbleen   -   a Strathspey

Old

Johnny Lad   -   a Reel

O if I were where Gadie runs - or the Hessian's March

Lassie an' Siller an' a's my ain

Mill O' Tiftie's Annie

Miss Boyd's Strathspey

Wm Christie

Ha'd the Cradle Rockin - a Reel

Old

Lady Dunbar of Northfield's Strathspey

Wm Christie

Lady Dunbar of Northfield's Reel

Wm Christie

Con Spirito

19

Dr Guthrie's (Junr) Strathspey

Wm Christie

Thro' the world wou'd I gang wi' the Lad that loves me - a Reel

Old

Maggie gae back an' tak' up your Scullie

Old

Slowly and distinctly

Communicated by Mr Jaffrey Senior

Willie are ye waukin - a Reel

Old

Mrs Gordon of Cairness' Strathspey

Wm Christie

Mrs Gordon of Cairness' Reel

Wm Christie

I'll hae a Piper to my Gudeman

Old

Slow

Communicated by J Allardyce

Mrs Gibbon's Strathspey

Wm Christie

Mrs Gibbon's Reel

Wm Christie

Pearlin Peggie's Bonny - or The Laird of Foveran

Old

Slow

Dolce

Mrs Dr Stewart's Strathspey

Wm Christie

*Slow when
not danced*

Mrs Dr Stewart's Reel

Wm Christie

Duncan Swine's Wife — a Strathspey

Old

Communicated by J Allardyce

The Clinkin o't — a Reel

Old

Mr Ritchie's Strathspey

Wm Christie

Mr Ritchie's Reel

Wm Christie

Fa's sae merry's the Miller when a' his Pocks are fu'

Old

Allegretto

The Waggle Cairn   -   a Strathspey

Wm Christie

Kind Robie come again   -   a Reel

Wm Christie

25

The Kail Reets of Fittie

Old

The Futterat wi' the gray tail   -   a Reel

Old

Miss Susan Brown's Strathspey

Wm Christie

Miss Louisa Brown's Reel

Wm Christie

Black at the Bane   -   a Strathspey

Slow when not danced

The Braes of Little Mill   -   a Reel

FINE

Mr McIntosh's Strathspey

Wm Christie

Slow when not danced

Mr McIntosh's Reel

Wm Christie

Vivace

Gather and go   -   a Jig

Old

Slowly and
Distinctly

Communicated by Mr Jaffrey Senior

Miss Cumine of Logie's Strathspey

Wm Christie

Miss Cumine of Logie's Reel

Wm Christie

I think the Carlie's wud the night   -   a Strathspey

Very Old

Kiss the Lass ye like best   -   a Reel

Lament for the Death of Hugh Allan

Wm Christie

Lento

Pathetic

cres.

p

cres.

Expn.

Mr Jaffrey's (Junr) Strathspey

Wm Christie

Robin fill the drink about — a Reel

Old

Miss Moodie's Hornpipe

Wm Christie

Good night and Joy be wi' you a'

Very Old

Andante

cres.

dolce

cres

30

Mrs Farquhar's Strathspey

Wm Christie

Mrs Farquhar's Reel

John Christie

The Bonny Banks of Ugie - a Strathspey

Wm Christie

Donald Simon   -   a Reel   Wm Christie

The World's gane o'er me now   -   a Jig   Old

Moderato

Communicated by J Allardyce

It's nae ay for want o' health the Ladies gang to Pannanich   -   a Reel

Lament for the Death of Lady Dunbar of Northfield   Wm Christie

Slow

Con Lamento   *cres.*   *Dolce*   *cres.*   *p*   *f*

32

Miss Kelman's Strathspey

Wm Christie

Miss Kelman's Reel

Wm Christie

The Humours of Cullen   -   a Jig

Smilin' Katie   -   a Reel

Mrs Peterkin of Grange Hall's Strathspey

Wm Christie

Mrs Peterkin of Grange Hall's Reel

Wm Christie

Fair an' Lucky

Very Old

Moderato

1.

2.

or

or

Mr Fletcher's Strathspey

Wm Christie

Mr Fletcher's Reel

by J. F.

The Finale – a Hornpipe

Wm Christie

Con Spirito

FINE

35

Thirty New

Strathspey Reels

For The

Violin or Harpsichord

Composed By

Isaac Cooper

Sold by James Imlach Bookseller Banff. And at R. Bremner's Music Shop Edin.

INDEX – ISAAC COOPER (1)

Lord Banff's Reel

Slow

Miss Henrietta Abernethie's Reel

Lieut. Abercromby's Reel

Miss Urquhart of Meldrum's Reel

Banff Castle

37

Mrs Rose's Reel

Miss Anny Forbes Reel

Mrs Geo. Abercromby's Reel

Mrs Doctor Abernethie's Reel

Miss Bettsy Robinson's Reel

Miss Bettsy Wilson's Reel

Miss Jeany Abernethie's Reel

Mrs Abercromby of Glassa's Reel

Miss Betty Forbes' Reel

Mrs James Duff's Reel

Miss Abernethie of Mayen's Reel

Miss Mary Urquhart's Reel

Miss Nancy Robinson's Reel

Miss Sophia Dirom's Reel

The Road to Down

Miss Innes of Edingight's Reel

The Harlequin Reel for the Violin

Up the Town in haste

In another copy of this there is a note "NB the Note with the tail turn'd up must be play'd with the 4th finger".

Miss Abercromby's Reel

Miss Dirom's Reel

Slow

41

Miss Gordon of Shieldagreen's Reel

Miss Herries Forbes Reel

Glassa House

Miss Gordon of Gight's Reel

Duff House

COLLECTION

of

Strathspeys, Reels,

and

IRISH JIGS,

for the

Piano Forte & Violin.

To which are added

Scots, Irish, & Welch Airs

Composed and Selected by

I. COOPER AT BANFF.

Price

Sold by the Music Sellers in London, Edinburgh, Aberdeen, Elgin, Inverness,

Glasgow and Stirling.

J. Johnson Sculp.t

INDEX- ISAAC COOPER (2)

The Dawning of Day - with Variations by I Cooper

Welch

N.B. The Violin is only to play the highest notes and not the Chords

The lake of Gold

Tweed Side

44

Ketty O'Ferrel

Irish

Miss Dirom   -   dancing Sett

Lord Banff   -   dancing Sett

Miss Ann Greigs Reel

I Cooper

Miss Ann Donaldsons Reel

I Cooper

Lady Charlotte Campbells New Reel

The Harlequin Strathspey   -   for the Violin

I Cooper

Up the Town in haste for the Violin

I Cooper

N.B. The note with the tail turn'd up must be play'd with the 4th finger

Miss Graham's Strathspey

Caper Fey

Carolanes Purse

Irish

Lord Banffs Strathspey

Isaac Cooper

Miss Diroms Strathspey

Isaac Cooper

Slow

Miss Bookers Reel

I Cooper

Banff Lasses   -   a Reel

I Cooper

50

Griegs Strathspey

Jarnovichs Reel

Carle can ye whistle

a very old tune

51

Callembruach   -   a Strathspey

Paddy O'Connor

Irish

The Irish Wedding

Dublin Key

Irish

Mullonies Jig

Irish

53

The Irish Lasses

Jacksons Hobby

Irish

Jacksons Folly

Irish

Not too quick

Jacksons Ramble

Irish

Not quick

The Wild Irishman

Paddy O'Rafferty

Irish

Teagues Ramble

Irish

Trafalgar - Strathspey

I Cooper

Slow

The Death of Nelson

Slow

I Cooper

The Victory   -   a Reel

I Cooper

A Bass to the Victory for the Violoncello

N.B. When two Violins play the Victory the 1st and 3rd Strains may be Play'd together

56

Mrs Gordon of Aberdour's Strathspey

I Cooper

The Marquis of Huntly's Highland Fling

Miss Sutton   -   a Reel

Dainty Davie   -   a Strathspey

The Rising of the Lark

58

The Dukers of Doon - a Strathspey

The Merry Lads of Clyde

Mrs Abernethy's Strathspey

I Cooper

Miss Isabella Reid's Reel

I Cooper

Mrs James Duffs Strathspey

I Cooper

Mrs Rose's Strathspey

I Cooper

Mrs Capt. Reid's Strathspey

I Cooper

viol

The Spell   -   a Reel

Miss Jane Gordons Reel

I Cooper

Miss G Abernethies Strathspey

I Cooper

Miss Gordon of Nethermuir's Strathspey *

I Cooper

* Originally called Miss Urquhart of Meldrum

Mrs Colquhoun Grants Strathspey

I Cooper

Miss Rose's Strathspey

I Cooper

62

Miss Forbes's Farewell to Banff

I Cooper

Mrs Grant   -   Dancing Set

The Lay's of Lunkerty   -   a Strathspey

Mrs Crombies Reel

I Cooper

Mr And. Laughlan's Welcome to Banff

I Cooper

64

Mr Willm. Fordyce's Strathspey

I Cooper

The Millar of Drone   -   altered by I Cooper

65

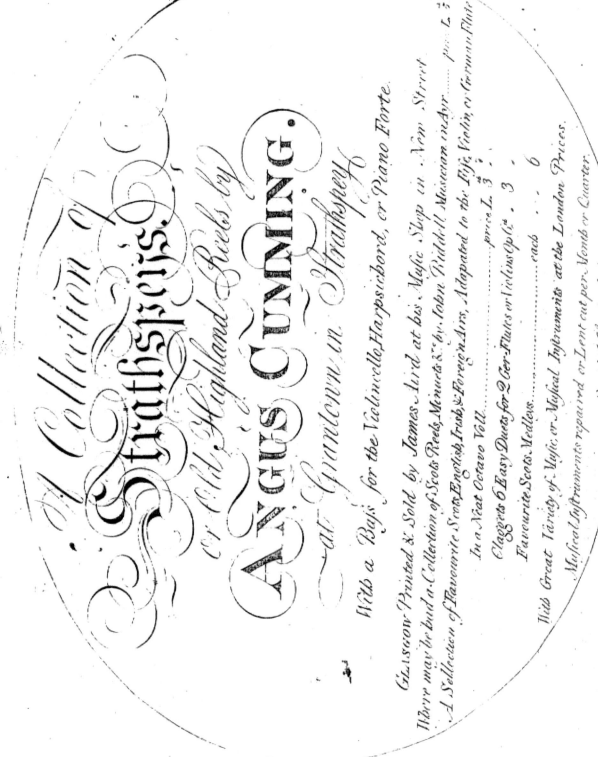

A Collection of

Strathspeys.

or Old Highland Reels by

ANGUS CUMMING.

at Grantown in Strathspey

With a Bass for the Violincello Harpsichord, or Piano Forte.

Glasgow Printed & Sold by James Aird at his Music Shop in New Street
Where may be had a Collection of Scots Reels, Menuets &c by John Riddell Musician in Ayr ——— price L. 3 :
A Selection of Favourite Scots English Irish, & Foreign Airs, Adapted to the Fife, Violin, or German Flute
In a Neat Octavo Voll. ——— price L. 3 :
Flaggets 6 Easy Duets for 2 Ger-Flutes or Violins Op.l.ⁱᵉ . 3
Favourite Scots Medleys ——— each . . 6

With Great Variety of Music or Musical Instruments at the London Prices.
Musical Instruments repaired or Lent out per Month or Quarter

Engraved by F. Johnson Edinburgh

INDEX – ANGUS CUMMING

Craig Elachie

The Fir Tree

The Grant's Rant - or Feve feve Tunal Chie

Lady Grant of Grants Reell - or Bog in Lochan

Acharnac's Reell - or Ba'l nan Grantich

Seme Rune Tallanach

Delachaple's Reel - or Bha mi Nrior nam carisk

Tullochgorm's Reel

The Dutchess of Hamiltons Reell - or Coigna Scalan

Dutchess of Buccleugh's Reell

Dutchess of Gordon's Reell - or Cean Loch Alain

Dutchess of Athole's Reell - or Tuggin tachi nul 'n Aird

Lady McIntosh's Reell

Lord Lovate's Reell - or Paal Mor

71

Sir Alexr Macdonald's Reell

Lady Grant of Dalvey's Reell

Lady Grant of Monymusk's Reell

72

Ballendalloch's Reell

Rothemurches's Reell - or Tigh 'ndun

Sir James Colquhoun's Reell

73

Arndilly's Reell - or Rittac air Mac'homaich

Lord Finlater's Reell

Rise lazy Lubber - or Erich buit erich

Lord Seaforth's Reell - or Thuar u Urrim chosen u a

Knockandoe's Reell - or Tom Neam

The Lass Amongst the Actenoch - or Nian a Bhodich sin rinattin

The Wedding - or San Rire va Vannich

The Bride - or Phit deubh

Dr Wm Grant's Reell - or Shaun Truish Willihan

Invercald's Reell

Corrimonie's Reell - or Keam Dulnich

The Sport - or Sanriar abhog a Fiannach

Whistle o'er the lave o't

The Forbes's Rant - or Don Side

The Bishop

General Grant's Reell - or Bal n' Iden

Macleod's Reell

77

Raza's Reell

Glen Morisone's Reell

Macpherson's Rant

The Cumming's Rant - or Reell of Tulloch   with Variations

Beggar's Bennison - or Thannie na buecht. horo

Lurg's Reell

The Monro's Rant - or Mal ro

Haugh's of Cromdale

80

The last pint - or Pint leur chine

Miss Grant of Grants Reell - or Rittal ar an Urlar

Lord Fife's Reell

Maclachlan's Reell

Carron's Reell - or U Choira Chruim

Kilravock's Reell

Mulchard's Dream - or Bruarthar Feare Mulachaird

The Millers Wedding

Sir Harry Innes's Reell

Glengerrie's Reell

Strathglass House - or The Chisholm's Reell

Clurie's Reell

Lethen's Reell

Shogallie's Reell

Miss Mary Grant's Reell

STRATHSPEYS,

REELS, - - -

PIBROCHS, &

MARCHES -

COMPOSED BY

CHAS. GRANT, M.A.,

Born at Strondhu, Knockando, 1810.

Died at Aberlour, 1892.

Thomson & Duncan, Printers, Aberdeen.

INDEX – CHARLES GRANT

The Braes of Elchies

Miss Sophia E Grant

Reel

Scurran-a-Wells

Strathspey

Mrs George Stewart's Strathspey

A Reel

Mrs Seller's Favourite, Dunleigh House

Lament for Mr Thomas Grant, of Glen Elgin

Andante

The Auld Kirk of Macallan

Reel

John Hay Deldonald

Strathspey

Corhabbie

Reel

87

Glenrinnes

Strathspey

Railway Hornpipe

Swiss Cottage   (Ballindalloch)

Reel

Mrs Duff, The Manse, Grange

Reel

Leggiero

p

mf

f

Miss Ann Gordon, Heath Cottage

Lament for Sir John Macpherson Grant

Miss Jeannie S Grant's Favourite

Mrs McMillan's Quadrillle

Craig-a-Chrochan - or Bridge of Ballindalloch

Strathspey

The Grants' Hornpipe

Mrs Bremner, The Manse, Glenbucket

Reel

Wester Elchies

Reel

I hae a lass o' my ain - or Mrs Grant

Miss Scott's Favourite March

Macallan

Strathspey

Mrs Professor Christie's Waltz

Scurran-a-Morange

Strathspey

Mrs Grant of Glen Grant

Reel

Glen Grant

Strathspey

Mrs Jamieson's Favourite

The South Side of Spey

Reel

93

Miss McMillan's Quadrille

A Reel

Skirdustan

Strathspey

94

James McInnes Esq. Dandaleith

Strathspey

The North Side of Spey

Strathspey

A Strathspey

Lynn Burn

Strathspey

Lament for the Auld Gean Tree of Wester Elchies

The Fairy Hillock

A pipe tune

Benrinnes

Strathspey

Mrs Forsyth's Pibroch (Manse of Abernethy)

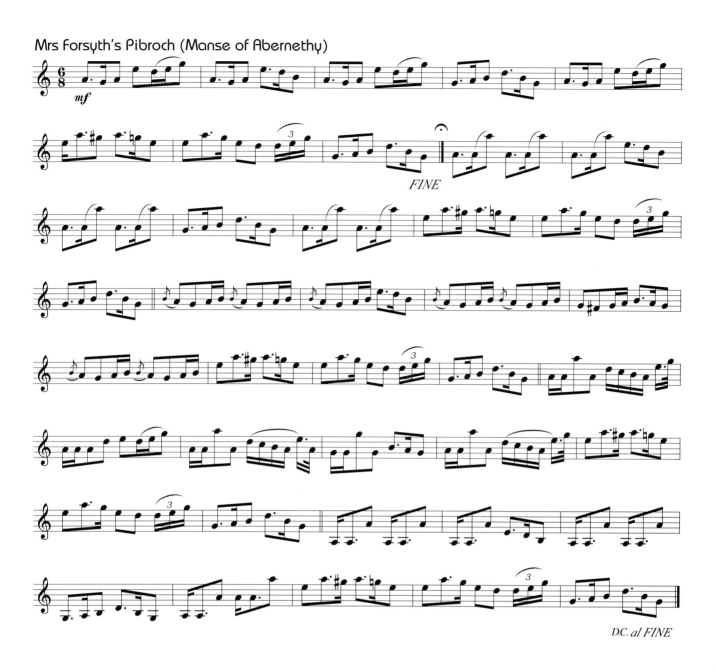

FINE

D.C. al FINE

97

Highland Wedding, Old

with variations

FINE

1st Var

2nd Var

3rd Var

4th Var

D.C. al FINE

Henry A Grant Esq. of Elchies

Strathspey

A Strathspey

Lynn of Ruthrie

A Reel

Ruthrie

Reel

Mrs Stephen Buchromb's Waltz

Aberlour Rifle Volunteer March

Edinvillie

Strathspey

Mr Thomas A Grant of Glen Elgin, Australia

Poolachrie

Dellagyle Pool

Reel

Kinermony

Strathspey

James McInnes Esq. Dandaleith

Reel

A

COLLECTION

of

Strathspeys, Reels, Jigs &c.

for the

PIANO FORTE, VIOLIN & VIOLONCELLO

Dedicated to

Mrs. Col. Grant of Grant

by

DONALD GRANT

The brave M'Intoshs and M'Kays
Some at Moudeole they did raise
they harried and fought most manfully
Upon the heughs of Cromdale

EDINBURGH.

Printed for the Author & to be had of him at Elgin & M'Gun, N° 47 Princes Street, Edinburgh & Innes, Henderson & M'Lellan, Inverness.

INDEX – DONALD GRANT

TO MRS COL. GRANT OF GRANT

MADAM - This Collection of Strathspeys, Reels, Jigs &c. is most humbly inscribed to you by the Publisher, as the only token
in his power whereby to acknowledge the high estimation in which he holds your patronage and good wishes: he is also proud to
acknowledge the no less distinguished patronage and generous kindness conferred on him, at an early period, by the late worthy,
and ever to be lamented Sir James and Lady Grant of Grant.

In hopes that his efforts, to add to the Stock of National Music, will have a happy tendency to meet your approbation, with that of
your numerous friends and the Public,

I have the honor to be, with Respect, MADAM,

Your much Obliged and most humble Servt.

D. GRANT

The Haughs of Cromdale   -   a Strathspey   Old

The Hills of Cromdale   -   a Reel   Old

Mrs Grant of Seabank's Strathspey   Donald Grant

Mr Alexr. Leslie's Strathspey

D Grant

FINE

Hard to the bone   -   a Strathspey

Very Old

The Banks of Nairn   -   a Reel

Old

104

Delrachnay's Rant

Old

Miss Fraser of Stoneyfield's Reel

Old

Orton House   -   a Strathspey

Old

She's Sweetest when she's Naked   -   a Reel

Old

FINE

Mrs Watt's Strathspey

Old

Mr Watt's Reel

Old

Mrs Col. Grant of Grant's Strathspey

D Grant

Mrs Col. Grant's Reel

D Grant

Miss Ross's Strathspey

D Grant

Mr Fortath's Reel

D Grant

Slowly when not danced

Miss Charlotte Ross's Reel

D Grant

Lady Dunbar of Boath's Strathspey

D Grant

This tune may be played Slow

Miss Wedderburn's Reel

Old

Mrs Fortath's Strathspey

D Grant

Slowly

The Earl of Seafield's Strathspey

D Grant

The Earl of Seafield's Reel

D Grant

Mrs Grant of Bught's Jig

Old

General Grant's Strathspey

Old

Miss Margt. Gordon's Reel

D Grant

Miss Shand's Strathspey

D Grant

Miss Mary Shand's Reel

D Grant

Munro's Rant

Old

The Banks of Spey

Very Old

110

Col. Grant of Grant's Strathspey

D Grant

Cullen House - a Reel

D Grant

The Deserts of Tulloch

Old

Mr McAndrew's Strathspey

D Grant

Slowly

111

Mrs Johnston's Reel

D Grant

Leiut. Col. Baillie of Leys Strathspey

James Anderson of Inverness

Miss Leslie of St Andrews Reel

D Grant

Mrs Fraser of Culbockie's Jig

Old

Mr Jas Thomson's Strathspey

D Grant

Mrs Fraser of Belladrum's Reel

Old

Mrs Rose of Kilravock's Jigg

Old

Mr Allan Grant's Strathspey

D Grant

Slowly

Miss Williamson of Oldfield's Jigg

Old

Charles Leslie of Findrassie's Strathspey

D Grant

Mrs Alexr. Brodie's Reel

Old

Mr McPhadden's Favorite

Old

Miss Jane Campbell's Strathspey

D Grant

Mr Sinclair younger of Barrack's Reel

Old

Mr Chas Gordon's Strathspey

D Grant

Dear Meal is cheap again   -   a Reel

Old

115

Mr Niel's Strathspey

Old

Mrs Grant of Laggan's Favorite

D Grant

Mrs Reid of Kilcalmkill's Strathspey

D Grant

Mr Reid's Reel

D Grant

Mrs Col. Sinclair of Forss's Strathspey

D Grant

Miss Munro of Dornoch's Reel

D Grant

His Grace the Duke of Gordon's Recovery

D Grant

Slowly

Miss Jane Grant of Grant's Reel

D Grant

Arndilly House   -   a Strathspey

D Grant

Slowly

Miss Macdowall Grant's Reel

D Grant

Lord Fife's welcome to Elgin

D Grant

Slowly

The Elgin Trinity Lodge's Strathspey

D Grant

The Keel Row   -   a Reel

Old

Mr Brander of Springfield's Strathspey

D Grant

Miss Henderson of Stempster's Reel

Old

Mrs Spence's Strathspey

D Grant

Mr Wm Young's Reel

D Grant

Miss Grant of Grant's Favorite

D Grant

Slowish

Lady Dunbar of Northfield's Strathspey

D Grant

Miss Jane Dunbar's Reel

D Grant

Castle Grant

Very Old

Miss Grant of Grant's Strathspey

Slowly

D Grant

121

Miss Rose of Tarlogie's Reel

Old

Mr Brander of Pitgavney's Strathspey

D Grant

Miss Brander's Reel

D Grant

Miss Penuel Grant of Grant's Strathspey

D Grant

Miss Jane Stewart's Reel

Old

Mr Lauder Dick's Strathspey

D Grant

Mrs Wilson's Reel

Mr Laughlan

Sir Archd. Dunbar of Northfield's Strathspey

D Grant

123

Miss Rose of Dranie's Reel

Old

The Bridegroom greets when the Sun gaes tee

Old

Slow

Mr Young of Maryhill's Strathspey

D Grant

Miss Taylor's Reel

D Grant

Darnway Castle - a Strathspey

D Grant

Miss Nicholson's Reel

D Grant

Lady Gordon Cumming's Strathspey

D Grant

Miss Sophia Cumming's Reel

D Grant

Hey the hedrie Falie   -   or Miss Brodie of Brodie's Favorite

Old

Mr Patrick Duff Junrs. Strathspey

D Grant

Mrs McInnes of Danalieth's Reel

Old

Mrs Henderson of Aimster's Favorite

D Grant

Miss Dunbar of Northfield's Strathspey

D Grant

The Earl of Moray's Reel

D Grant

Miss Duff of Muirton's Jig

Old

Mrs Col. Hay of Mayne's Strathspey

D Grant

Mrs Masson's Reel

D Grant

Miss Brown of Linkwood's Strathspey

D Grant

Mrs Anderson of Kincraig's Strathspey

D Grant

128

Mr Reid of Elgin Academy's Strathspey

D Grant

Mrs Dr. Stephen's Reel

D Grant

The Marchioness of Huntly's Strathspey

D Grant

The Marquis of Huntly's Reel

D Grant

Rothiemurchus

Original Set

Miss Grant of Elchies's Strathspey

D Grant

I Lost my heart on Friday   -   a Reel

Old

Moonmore's Strathspey

Old

Mrs Dr Torrence of Thurso's Reel

Old

Col. Alexr. Grant's Strathspey - or New Sweet Molly

D Grant

Mr Robt. Bain's Strathspey

D Grant

Mrs Grant of Viewfield's Reel

Old

Mr McDonald of Gordon Castle's Strathspey

D Grant

Prior's   -   or Mr Malie's Strathspey

Old

132

Mrs General Stewart's Strathspey

D Grant

Mrs Gordon of Moonmore's Strathspey

D Grant

Mr Duncan of Garmouth's Strathspey

D Grant

Mrs Walker of Urquhart's Strathspey

D Grant

Dr Wm Grigor of Elgin's Reel

D Grant

Major Ray's Strathspey

D Grant

Mr P Brown of Linkwood's Strathspey

D Grant

Mrs Major Ray's Favorite

D Grant

Miss Gordon's Reel

Old

135

EIGHT AIRS

FOR

VIOLIN

with Pianoforte Accompaniment

Composed by

JAMES HENRY.

Price Two Shillings net.

LONDON
BAYLEY & FERGUSON
2, Great Marlborough St. W.
Glasgow, 54 Queen Street.

INDEX - JAMES HENRY

Romance

The Auld Brig o' Don   -   Solo strathspey

Robert Carmack   -   Pastoral strathspey

George Taylor - Hornpipe

James Morrison - Strathspey

James Morrison - Reel

George Wright   -   Strathspey

Miss Isabella Carle   -   Reel

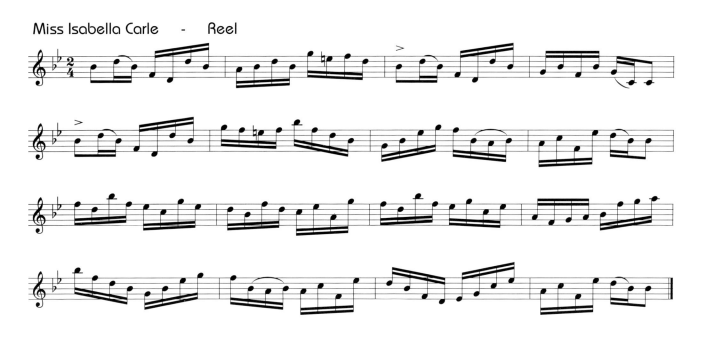

A

COLLECTION OF

Highland Music,

CONSISTING OF

Strathspeys Reels Marches Waltzes & Slow Airs

WITH *Variations* ORIGINAL & *Selected* FOR THE

PIANO FORTE

Violin AND Violoncello

Dedicated to the Right Honble

Lady Seaforth

BY

William Morrison

PRICE   ENTERED AT STATIONERS HALL.   7/6

Printed for & Sold by J. Young & Co. Inverness and to
be had of all Music Sellers

INDEX – WILLIAM MORRISON

TO THE RIGHT HON: LADY SEAFORTH

I Beg leave with the utmost deference to lay before your Ladyship this Collection of STRATHSPEYS, REELS,
WALTZES and SLOW AIRS etc ORIGINAL and SELECT, being the only means in my power (however inadequate)
to evince the unfeigned sensations of gratitude with which I feel impressed on account of the numerous favours and early
protection which I have experienced under your Ladyships much esteemed patronage.

Should therefore these my humble exertions (being my first attempt of the kind) be honored with your Ladyships kind
approbation and that of a generous and discerning Public, the object of my ambition is completely secured, which I shall
ever be proud to acknowledge, while I have the honor to be your Ladyships most grateful Obedient and humble Servant.

WILLIAM MORRISON

S'irom trom a tha mi - or Sad Sad am I

A Favourite Highland Air, The second strain by W Morrison

Caper Fey

Culloden House

J Anderson

Culloden Well

W Morrison

Lady Gordon of Gordonstown's Strathspey

W Morrison

142

Lady Gordon of Gordonstown's Reel

W Morrison

North of the Grampians

Capt. Fraser

Laing and Hendry's Birth Day - or the 4th of April

W Morrison

Miss Ann Robinson's Strathspey

W Morrison

Capt. Young of Banff's Reel

W Morrison

The Four Following Tunes Composed by a Gentleman *
A March for the Clans

* *Of whose numerous acts of experienced humanity, the Author of this Collection shall ever retain the most lively sensations of gratitude*

Muirtown House

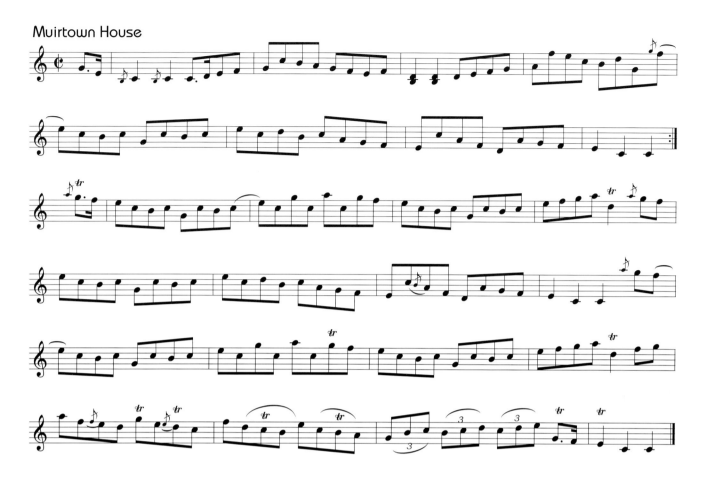

W Morrison's Favorite

The Peramble

Peter Reid Esqr. Kinardy

W Morrison

Mr Meldrum's Reel, Banff

146

Mrs Duff's Recovery

The Ladys of Dingwall   -   a Reel

Tulloch Castle   -   a Strathspey

by a Lady

Loch Madey   -   a Reel

by a Gentleman

Mrs McLeod Younger of Talasker's Strathspey

W Morrison

Lady McKinzie of Coul's Reel

Mr McLeod of Rasey

148

Culloden's Favorite

W Morrison

Mr Campbell of the Academay's Strathspey

Are you always pleased

The variations by W Morrison

The 2 Last Variations by W Morrison

151

Mrs Ross, Dowger of Kilravock's Favorite

A Jinkins

Marquis (of) Willington

Mrs Andrew's Strathspey

W Morrison

152

Alexr Arthur Duff Esqr Younger of Muirtown's Reel

W Morrison

The Bachelors Jig

W Morrison

Allegro

Mr Morrison Supervisor Dingwall   -   Reel

W Morrison

Lady Jane Montagues Strathspey

W Morrison

Viscount Mandeville

W Morrison

Mr Wagstaffs Favorite

W Morrison

Slow

W Morrison's Compliments to Mr Scott 78th Regt. Band

Miss Amelia Mary Duff of Muirtown's Strathspey

W Morrison

Mr Duncan Forbes Duff of Muirtown's Reel

W Morrison

155

Mr Wm Eccles Favorite

W Morrison

Slow & Distinct

Mr Gibb's Jig

J Boick

Miss Bowis of Inverness - Strathspey

W Morrison

Dr Ross of Dornoch - a Reel

W Morrison

Mrs Duff of Muirtown's Waltz

W Morrison

Miss Sarah Georgiana Duff of Muirtown's Strathspey

W Morrison

Murphey Dellany

the 3rd Strain by W Morrison

This Tune may be played for a Bumpkin

Mad Cap - Reel

W Morrison

D.S.

Tibby Fowler's Grand Daughter, or the Bother - Strathspey

W Morrison

Capt H Munro of Newtown's Reel

W Morrison

Riefield Lodge - Strathspey

W Morrison

Black Strap - Reel

W Morrison

* Oigfhear a chulduinn   -   The Brown Hair'd Youth

A St Kilda Song

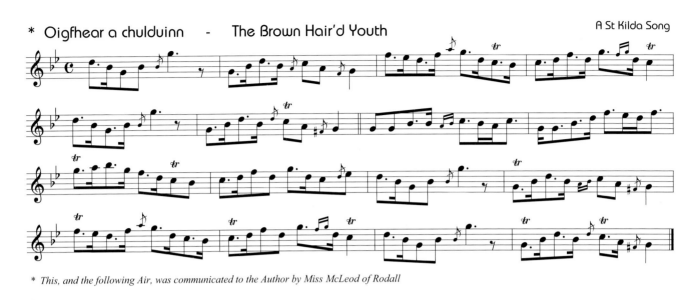

* This, and the following Air, was communicated to the Author by Miss McLeod of Rodall

Horuinn o u oro

A St Kilda Air

O mo chuid chuideachda, O thou my choice of Companions *

* by a Highland Sportsman to his Gun.   The three Last Strains by W Morrison

160

Mrs Mcleod of Geastow's Strathspey

W Morrison

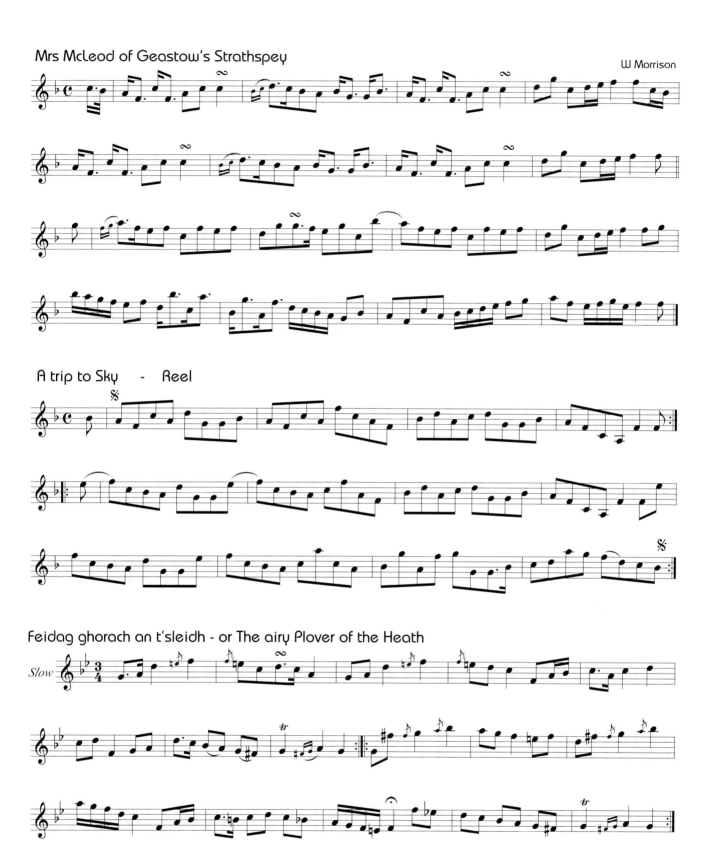

A trip to Sky - Reel

Feidag ghorach an t'sleidh - or The airy Plover of the Heath

Slow

Mrs McLeod of Rasey's Strathspey

W Morrison

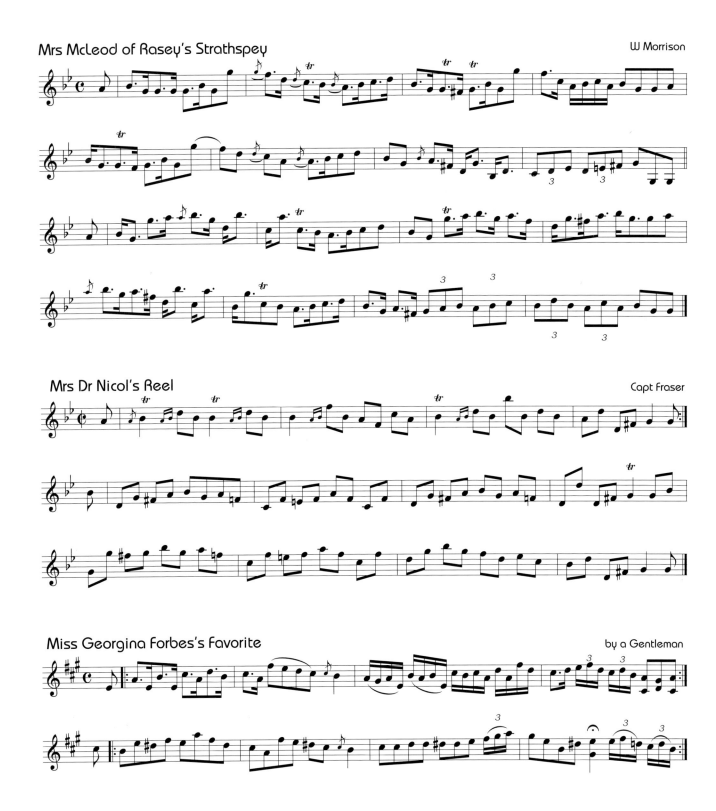

Mrs Dr Nicol's Reel

Capt Fraser

Miss Georgina Forbes's Favorite

by a Gentleman

Culloden Waltz

W Morrison

Lady Hood's Favorite

W Morrison

Hornpipe time

Squital Bridge

W Morrison

Lewis Gordon

the Variations by W Morrison

Inverness - or The Northern Meeting

W Morrison

164

Brahan Castle

The Hon. Miss Charlotte McKinzie's Favorite

W Morrison

FINE

D.S.

A Gallop to Kinross

D McDonald

A Trip to Strathbogie

D McDonald

Culloden Muir

W Morrison

Slow

166

The Hon. Mr McKinzie of Seaforth's Birth Day   -   Reel

W Morrison

Miss Christian Duff's Favorite

by a Gentleman

Slow

Mr H R Duff's Favorite

by a Gentleman

FINE

D.S.

Mrs Lumsden of Achindore's Reel

Mr Marshall

Geordie Afflick   -   Reel

Lament for the Death of Jane Duchess of Gordon

D McDonald

Slow with Expression

St John's Well

C Bleaw

168

Lady Mary Ross's Favorite

W Morrison

The Western Harvest Home

Mrs McLean of Borrowry's Strathspey

W Morrison

Robt. Abercromby Esqr. M.P   -   Reel

W Morrison

Sleep on till Day

Slow with Expression

INDEX